Beyond the Hoppo Ryodo

Japanese-Soviet-American Relations in the 1990s

Jo Dee Catlin Jacob
Editor

The AEI Press

Publisher for the American Enterprise Institute
WASHINGTON, D.C.

1991

Distributed by arrangement with

University Press of America, Inc.
4720 Boston Way   3 Henrietta Street
Lanham, Md. 20706   London WC2E 8LU England

Library of Congress Cataloging-in-Publication Data

Beyond the Hoppo Ryodo : Japanese—Soviet—American relations in the
    1990s / Jo Dee Catlin Jacob, editor.
        p.   cm. — (Special analysis : 91-2)
    ISBN 0-8447-7009-4 : $7.95
        1. United States—Foreign relations—Japan.   2. Japan—Foreign
    relations—United States.   3. Japan—Foreign relations—Soviet
    Union.   4. Soviet Union—Foreign relations—Japan.   5. United
    States—Foreign relations—Soviet Union.   6. Soviet Union—Foreign
    relations—United States.   7. United States—Foreign
    relations—1989–   8. Japan—Foreign relations—1945–   9. Soviet
    Union—Foreign relations—1985–   10. Kurile Islands (R.S.F.S.R.)
    I. Jacob, Jo Dee Catlin.   II. Series: AEI special analyses : 91-2.
    E183.8.J3B52   1991
    327.73052—dc20   90-26233
                                                                    CIP

1 3 5 7 9 10 8 6 4 2

AEI Special Analyses 91-2

Printed in the United States of America

Contents

Contributors

Jo Dee Catlin Jacob, editor, is military faculty member at the National Defense University. She was 1989–1990 navy fellow at the American Enterprise Institute. An education and training specialist and unrestricted line officer, Commander Jacob spent fifteen years with the Pacific Fleet.

Donald C. Hellmann is professor of international studies and political science at the Henry M. Jackson School of International Relations, University of Washington. He writes widely on Japanese foreign policy and on the international relations of East Asia. Mr. Hellmann is a member of the Council of Academic Advisers of the American Enterprise Institute.

John H. Makin is resident scholar and director of Fiscal Policy Studies at the American Enterprise Institute. He was professor of economics and director of the Institute for Economic Research, University of Washington. Mr. Makin has written and edited numerous books on fiscal policy issues and U.S.-Japanese relations, including *Sharing World Leadership? A New Era for America and Japan.* He is a member of the Congressional Budget Office's Panel of Economic Advisers and an associate editor of Harvard University's *Review of Economics and Statistics.*

Rajan Menon is associate professor of international relations at Lehigh University. As international affairs fellow and special assistant for arms control and national security for the Council on Foreign Relations, Mr. Menon specialized in Soviet foreign policy. His books include *Limits to Soviet Power* and *Soviet Power and the Third World.*

WILLIAM T. PENDLEY is director for strategic planning and policy, U.S. Pacific Command. A naval aviator and political-military specialist, Rear Admiral Pendley is responsible for developing U.S. military strategies and economic policy in the Pacific. He served as commander of U.S. naval forces in Korea and as senior member of the UN Command Military Armistice Commission.

RICHARD N. PERLE is resident fellow and director of Defense Policy Studies at the American Enterprise Institute. As assistant secretary of defense for international security policy from 1981 to 1987, he was responsible for nuclear weapons policy and negotiations between the United States and its western allies and the Soviet Union. Mr. Perle is a member of the Defense Policy Board and a contributing editor of *U.S. News and World Report.*

VASILIY B. POSPELOV is third secretary at the Soviet embassy in Washington, D.C. His diplomatic assignments have included the Soviet embassy in Bangkok, the Ministry of Foreign Affairs (Department for South-East Asian Affairs), and the Bureau for Asian Socialist Countries (Democratic People's Republic of Korea, People's Republic of China, and Indochina).

MICHAEL POWELL is assistant for Japan in the office of the secretary of defense. A former army cavalry officer, he is responsible for formulating policy for the Department of Defense relating to the bilateral security alliance between the United States and Japan.

THOMAS W. ROBINSON is director of the China Studies Program at the American Enterprise Institute. He is also adjunct professor of China studies, government, and national security at Georgetown University and chairman of the Foreign Service Institute's Asian Studies Course since 1983. Mr. Robinson has published widely on Chinese politics and foreign policy, Soviet-Asian policy, and Asian international relations. He has taught at the National War College, Dartmouth College, Princeton and Columbia universities and has conducted extensive research at the RAND Corporation and the Council on Foreign Relations.

CONTRIBUTORS

MASARU TAMAMOTO, a Japanese national, is assistant professor at the School of International Service, American University. He was Mac-Arthur Foundation Visiting Fellow at Princeton University's Center of International Studies and conducted research at the Institute of Oriental Culture, University of Tokyo.

Foreword

Nowhere is the question Can we survive the end of the cold war? more compelling than in Northeast Asia. Occupied since 1945 by the Soviet Union and referred to by Japan as its Northern Territories (Hoppo Ryodo), four islands have for almost half a century confined Japanese-Soviet dialogue to brief, fruitless discussions of a return of these lands to Japan. Now, more than a year after the collapse of Soviet pretensions in Europe, the familiar formula whereby cash is exchanged for a Soviet retreat from territory apparently will be applied in Asia to settle this dispute with Japan.

In one sense the Soviet return of the Northern Territories to Japan will destabilize Japanese-Soviet relations. The territorial dispute will no longer define the dialogue between two of Asia's three great powers, one military and one economic. The potential for symbiosis between the capital-rich but resource-poor, land-poor Japan and the economically poor but resource-rich, expansive Soviet Union may seem great, but history says otherwise.

The past, present, and future of Japanese-Soviet relations are explored through this revealing prism of the Northern Territories issue in this special analysis prepared by AEI navy fellow, Jo Dee Catlin Jacob. Soviet, Japanese, and predominantly American third-party perspectives are included. The result is a compendium of views on relations between Japan, the United States, and the Soviet Union as settlement of the Northern Territories dispute marks the end of the postwar order in Asia. What follows will be fascinating to observe and undoubtedly will bear critically upon regional stability in the post–cold war era.

AEI is grateful to the Pew Charitable Trusts for generous support of the preparation of this special analysis under a grant to study Japanese-Soviet-American relations.

JOHN H. MAKIN

1

Introduction

Jo Dee Catlin Jacob

While East-West relations have improved, the symbols for Japanese-Soviet relations are a few cold, windswept islands in the North Pacific.
—ANDREW HORVAT, *The International Economy*

Japanese-Soviet relations, stalemated since 1945 over the Hoppo Ryodo (Northern Territories), show signs of thawing and may warm in time for President Mikhail Gorbachev's scheduled historic visit to Tokyo in the spring of 1991. What are the political, economic, and security implications for the United States if the Japanese and Soviets finally sit down and talk? Nine leading scholars, academicians, diplomats and U.S. defense officials consider the possibilities of Japanese-Soviet rapprochement in this volume. The analysts move beyond the Hoppo Ryodo dispute to issues that either inhibit or offer hope for normalization of relations between the long-time adversaries. Richard Perle, William Pendley, and Michael Powell comment from their policy-making experiences in national defense and regional security. The Soviet Embassy's Vasiliy Pospelov and Japanese academician Masaru Tamamoto offer personal insights from their respective homelands. Long-time Japan observers John Makin and Donald Hellmann urge new and different thinking to break loose the stalemate. Asia experts Thomas Robinson and Rajan Menon caution that any such rapprochement will affect the entire region.

To frame our analysis, it is valuable to mention the geography of the area and the history of Japanese-Soviet relations, especially as they pertain to the disputed islands.

At the far southwest tail of the Kurile Islands chain lie the Habomai Group, Shikotan, Kunashiri, and Etorofu, totaling 4,996

1

square kilometers. Just 3.7 kilometers off Hokkaido's Cape Nosappu, the islands at the conflux of warm and cold currents are found in some of the world's best fishing grounds.

The 1855 Treaty of Commerce, Navigation, and Delimitation between Japan and Russia established that these four islands were Japanese territory, distinct from the Kurile chain. Subsequent pacts including the 1875 Treaty for the Exchange of Sakhalin for the Kurile Islands, the 1905 Treaty of Portsmouth ending the Russo-Japanese War, and the Cairo Communique of 1943 reaffirmed the historical tradition that these Northern Territories belonged to Japan.

On August 8, 1945, just two days after the Hiroshima bombing, the USSR declared war on Japan and moved quickly to get a piece of the action in the Pacific. Although the well-equipped Japanese repelled the first Soviet amphibious assault, a subsequent order from Imperial Army Headquarters resulted in Japanese surrender.

The Yalta Agreement seems to be the fundamental document that the Soviets use to justify seizure of the Hoppo Ryodo. This document provided that the Kurile Islands would be handed over to the USSR after the war, but the names of the islands were not specified. Stalin took advantage of this oversight, or ignorance, and invaded the Northern Territories. Despite stipulations of the 1951 San Francisco Conference Peace Treaty, the 1956 Japanese-Soviet Joint Declaration, and American protests throughout the postwar period, the USSR evacuated the Japanese fishermen on the islands in 1945 and have continued to occupy the lands. Stationed on the islands and worrisome to Japan are Soviet MIG-23 Flogger fighters and troops equivalent to an army division.

Aggravating the feud, the Soviets have over the years seized more than a thousand boats and apprehended Japanese fishermen at work in the disputed territorial waters. Particularly irritating to the Japanese has been the Soviet refusal to permit exiled residents to visit their ancestors' graves.

From the Soviet perspective the islands are strategically important because they increase their ice-free access to the Pacific while inhibiting U.S. access to the Sea of Okhotsk. In addition to precious fishing prerogatives, the USSR does not wish to relinquish the Kuriles for fear of setting a precedent that could spill over to the Balkans by abrogating lands gained as war spoils. Moscow has inferred that the islands are perhaps not really that important to Tokyo, that Japan

2

uses the issue to avoid dealing with the USSR. Japanese politicians carefully cultivate anti-Soviet feelings and use the territorial issue as a nationalistic rallying cry to unite the voters.

As a result the Japanese and Soviets have never signed a peace treaty formally ending World War II. For forty-five years, the Japanese have steadfastly refused to negotiate without the return of the Hoppo Ryodo. The Soviets have just as stubbornly dismissed the issue of the Northern Territories as a closed book. Meeting after meeting has ended in stalemate because neither side would compromise.

The focus on the Kurile Islands issue veils a much darker historical enmity between Russia and Japan. The two empires competed fiercely for regional hegemony in the nineteenth century. Japanese strategists consciously decided against attacking the USSR at the outset of World War II, perhaps saving the Soviets for later. Mutual distrust has not changed since. The dispute over the Northern Territories has driven an economic and political wedge between the USSR and Japan at a time when the Soviets could greatly benefit from Japan's technological and industrial riches.

Signs of Thaw

Many Japan experts viewing the impending summit between Soviet President Gorbachev and Japanese Prime Minister Toshiki Kaifu discount the idea of an imminent peace treaty. "Japan will wait for guidance from the U.S. before it makes a move with the Russians," Masaru Tamamoto said. "Waiting for full-fledged rapprochement between Japan and the Soviet Union," Michael Powell observed, "is waiting for the unlikely." Nevertheless Japanese perceptions about the Soviet Union may be changing, and recent initiatives are notable:

• In September 1990 Soviet Foreign Minister Eduard Shevardnadze and his Japanese counterpart Taro Nakayama issued a rare joint communique condemning the Iraqi aggression in Kuwait. Although the document itself was otherwise routine diplomacy, that Tokyo and Moscow could come to any such agreement was noteworthy indeed.

• Facing the severe winter and critical shortages, Moscow appealed to Japan for emergency shipments of medical supplies, consumer goods, and food. Tokyo pledged $108 million in humanitarian aid to help the Soviets through the winter of 1991.

3

• In December 1990 television journalist Toyohiro Akiyama became the first Japanese astronaut by joining Soviet cosmonauts on a successful Soyuz-MIR space station mission.

• Japanese are now permitted to visit ancestral graves, albeit with USSR visas to remind them that the islands are indeed Soviet.

• Gorbachev outlined unprecedented new policy toward Asia during speeches delivered in Vladivostok in July 1986 and Krasnoyarsk in September 1988. In his texts he emphasized the importance of the region and even called Japan vital.

• During his November 1989 visit Soviet diplomat Alexander Yakovlev teased the Tokyo press with hints of a third solution to the problem of the Northern Territories. This innuendo takes on added significance because the Soviet minister's visit was in preparation for President Gorbachev's scheduled visit to Tokyo in 1991. This, the first visit of a Soviet head of state to Japan, is fertile ground for a dramatic, magnanimous gesture of rapprochement such as returning the Hoppo Ryodo.

In terms of investment, Japanese-Soviet industrial cooperation has been limited to high hopes and aborted attempts. Key among them was the ill-fated venture into Eastern Siberia in the 1970s, where the Japanese attempted to tap its estimated 700 trillion cubic feet of natural gas. Since then, the Japanese have developed trade markets in Thailand, the Philippines, and Indochina. Like the military strategists in 1940, Japanese economic strategists have decided to strike south instead of north.

The Soviet Union may be in an economic death spiral. To pull out of it, Japanese investment is a major target for hard cash and convertible currency. The USSR would certainly welcome the sophisticated technology and finished goods that Japan can deliver.

The U.S.-Japanese Alliance

Predictions that a Japanese-Soviet rapprochement would shake up the decades-old U.S.-Japanese alliance are unsettling. A public debate about the American military presence in Japan would be difficult for Japan's ruling Liberal Democratic party. The rationale for any increased defense spending would be questioned by opposition parties. Yet a qualitatively new relationship between the Soviet Union and Japan is doubtful. Such a conjecture radically departs from the conventional wisdom that the Japanese are staunchly anti-Communist.

Moreover, as Admiral Pendley points out, the long-standing common interests that underpin the unique security agreement between the United States and Japan—protectionism, regional balance, freedom of the seas, and democracy—make any abridgement of the Treaty of Mutual Cooperation and Security nearly unthinkable.

Despite any exaggeration of real concerns, rhetoric on potential problems in U.S.-Japanese relations is at an all-time high. Japan bashing and grousing about trade inequities have reached unprecedented levels, prompting John Makin to caution "the (Japanese-American) relationship is a crisis waiting to happen . . . and may be brought on by an extraneous event like Toshiba" selling critical defense technology to the Soviets.

Defense spending or burden sharing is another thorny issue between these long-time allies. Thriving under the protective umbrella of the American military for the past forty-five years, Japan is now an economic superpower. Except for significant political opposition, both at home and throughout Asia, Japan could fund a far greater share of its regional defense burden. The pressure from the American Congress for greater Japanese cost sharing is formidable, and Tokyo has felt the heat.

Yet some Japanese say they are already paying their full share. They feel unappreciated by their American benefactors for the significant contribution they do make ($2.57 billion per year for U.S. forces in Japan, or about $51,000 per man). Many Japanese feel that the Self-Defense Force is strong enough and that any further buildup would violate their constitution, a constitution written by the American occupation force after World War II.

If regional instability were its motives, Soviet timing could not be better for attempting to benefit from a rebound romance. Although Japanese-American relations since World War II have always been superb, they have deteriorated in recent years. An August 1989 Louis Harris poll showed that Americans perceive the economic challenge of Japan to be greater than the challenge of Soviet military might. This is especially significant since the poll reflected opinions *before* the Berlin Wall fell.

There is little disagreement that for the past half-century the U.S. presence in the area has been a stabilizing force in Asia. "The last thing the Soviets want is a Japan cut adrift from the United States," Rajan Menon explained. Donald Hellmann agreed: "Such a Japan would create at the very least, an unknown—a loose cannon, something that's out of control." Even Vasiliy Pospelov conceded that "the level of interdependence makes drastic change in U.S.-Japan relations impossible. Concerns that the Soviets will drive a wedge between the Americans and the Japanese are groundless."

On the political scene Japanese Prime Minister Kaifu is on record as encouraging glasnost, perestroika, and Gorbachev's desire to improve Japanese-Soviet relations. But he skillfully balances supporting Gorbachev's enlightened domestic policies and ensuring that Japan's security interests are protected. His Liberal Democratic party has reliably supported the U.S. alliance and has steadily increased defense expenditures. The Japan Socialist party, however, favors reduced reliance on U.S. technology, touts an agenda of reduced defense spending, and advocates renegotiating the Treaty of Mutual Cooperation and Security with the United States.

Rapprochement

What is the probability of near-term rapprochement? Predictions run from extremely small to likely and all points in between, many pivoting on the terms of resolving the Northern Territories dispute. Terms could include returning two islands now and negotiating for the other two later. Other terms could be conditioned on demilitarization of Japan, hard currency payments, or direct Japanese investment in the USSR.

Strategists recognize that a full-fledged rapprochement with the Japanese—this would be beyond the Soviets' fondest dreams—is unnecessary to achieve more sinister Soviet objectives; merely a wedge driven between the United States and Japan would suffice. U.S. contingency plans in the region are based on Japanese cooperation and operations from Japanese territory. Any interference with or restriction from using Japanese facilities would reduce U.S. joint military options in the theater.

The impact of decreasing the Soviet threat, as represented by the possibility, let alone reality, of returning the Hoppo Ryodo, could cause a public clamor for reduced defense spending. An important public relations issue, both Washington and Tokyo are justifiably concerned that Soviet intentions not be confused with Soviet capabilities. If the Soviet threat to Japan is perceived to be decreasing, Liberal Democratic party incumbents will have difficulty justifying increased defense spending. Certainly the same sentiments are shared in the American Congress.

Yet clearly Gorbachev has more pressing issues than resolving the Northern Territories dispute. In the past it was difficult to determine the place of Japanese-Soviet relations on the list of Soviet foreign policy priorities. Moreover there is as yet no ground swell of support in Japan for a dramatic shift in relations with the Soviets. According to Andrew Horvat, Tokyo bureau, *London Independent*, only 3 percent of Japanese find the USSR especially trustworthy.

As for the territorial claim, Japan may prefer the problem to the solution. Over the years Japan's high principle on this issue has facilitated its status quo of distant relations with the Soviets, while thriving under the protective U.S. security umbrella.

Certainly unconditional return of the Hoppo Ryodo should be the objective of the Japanese. It is in their best interests politically, economically, and strategically.

The Land of the Rising Sun has waited for her family reunion half a century and appears to be in no hurry to negotiate anything less than a complete victory. With its cash, technology, industrial might, and beneficial military alliance, Japan is at the helm when it comes to dealing with the Soviets. Thus far, she has chosen to stay tied up at the pier.

Early in 1990, amid a restless Russian crowd impatient with its faltering economy, Gorbachev announced to the watching world that he needed two years for his perestroika to work. But that is not enough time to reverse the ravaging effects of seventy-five years of communism. In two years, if he wants to stay in office, Gorbachev may need a massive infusion of Western currency or a rabbit in the hat.

The Hoppo Ryodo and Japanese investment in the USSR could be his rabbit in the hat. If the 1991 Tokyo summit goes beyond the Hoppo Ryodo and Gorbachev returns the Northern Territories to Japan, prospects may be bright for serious negotiations between Japan and the Soviet Union.

2
Ready to Talk

Vasiliy B. Pospelov

Despite the fascination of this subject there is a danger to engage in pure speculations. It is difficult to predict the character of Soviet-Japanese relations in the next decade and its possible global and regional impact. Too many variables affect the dynamics of this relationship. The pace of change will be derived by many internal and external factors.

In recent years the place of relations with Japan on the list of Soviet foreign policy priorities was uncertain. On one hand, Moscow understood that, taking into account Japanese economic potential and the growing role played by Japan in world politics, its relations with Japan are very important. Japanese economic involvement in Eastern Europe, the prospects for changes in Indochina, Mongolia, and Korea made the Soviet Union increasingly interested not only in broadening its bilateral ties with Japan, but in achieving mutual understanding and some degree of cooperation with her.

On the other hand, despite the attention paid to Soviet-Japanese relations, events in Eastern Europe, the breakthroughs in Soviet-American and Soviet-Chinese relations, the emergence of a united Germany, and a completely new structure of security arrangements in Europe somewhat overshadow Soviet relations with its eastern neighbor. As the Japanese were reluctant to take the initiative, Soviet-Japanese relations remained practically untouched by perestroika.

I offer these thoughts in my private capacity as an orientalist specializing in North Asian affairs. My remarks are by no means an official policy statement but rather some reflections on the subject of Soviet relations with Japan.

Now the situation has started to change. Although the Soviet-Japanese normalization is only one of many international problems faced by Moscow and Tokyo, both sides apparently have realized that the current standoff does not benefit either of them and further delay in positive actions would be detrimental to their interests.

There are some basic principles in Soviet policy toward Japan. The USSR does not have one policy for Europe and another for Asia or Japan. Soviet policy toward Japan is guided by the same principles of new political thinking that is applied to relations with the United States or Europe. Although in this century the Russians and the Soviets fought three wars against Japan, there is no bias against the Japanese. Moreover the approach of the Soviet public toward Japan, as manifested in polls, is very positive. Japan ranks among the top three countries in the sympathy of the Soviet people.

The USSR is seeking real improvement in relations with Japan and thinks that it is quite possible. In today's world there is no room for geopolitical games. The Soviet Union will not try to contain Japan, to deter it, or to weaken its position. Just the opposite, we consider emerging multipolarity in the world as a positive phenomenon consistent with the principles of democratization of international relations and greater stability and balance in world politics.

The Soviet Union fully accepts and supports increasing the political role of Japan in the world, be it in the United Nations, Eastern Europe, Latin America, Indochina, Middle East or elsewhere. We welcome Japan's intention to participate in United Nations peacekeeping operations. Gone are the times when Japan's attempts to establish economic relations or provide assistance, say, to Vietnam or Mongolia, were seen as capitalist infiltration. Now the Soviet side appreciates Japan's contribution to economic recovery of Socialist countries. Our only reservation is that Japanese development assistance not be used as direct leverage to obtain certain political goals. In general the USSR has no problem with the new Japanese role in the world, and there is no room for conflict between the Soviet and American approaches to it.

Our view of Japan's military potential is also clear. The Soviet Union fully respects Japan's right to a reasonable defense sufficiency. Although certain political forces in Japan would like to turn Japan into a military superpower, we have no reason to doubt the choice made by the Japanese people to be a peaceful nation, which is embodied in their constitution. The democratic institutions in Japan seem to be strong enough to make a turn toward some kind of militaristic, aggressive regime not viable. After all, Japan first set an example of becoming a superpower without major military forces, and no external or internal trends that could push Japan against the tide of history are visible.

But the Soviet side remains strongly opposed to Japan's exceeding the limits of a reasonable defense sufficiency. In defining these limits, the objective reality—including the existence of a U.S.-Japanese military alliance—should be taken into account. Otherwise a new vicious circle of the arms race could start in the region.

In this context we are sensitive to the exaggerated assessment of the Soviet military posture that seems to prevail in Japan. Overestimating the Soviet threat to Japan might serve as a pretext for a dangerous Japanese military buildup which can destabilize Asia.

In economic relations the USSR is interested in cooperation with Japan. But it would be a mistake to think that we will not be able to manage without Japanese participation. The core problem in the Soviet economy is its mechanism and not the lack of foreign investment. If economic reforms are successful and a new mechanism placed in order, the Soviet economy will develop with or without Japanese involvement. The strategic importance of our resources in Siberia and the Far East will not diminish in the long run. And in the years ahead Japan will meet strong competition for access to these resources. Given our geographical proximity, however, the absence of strong economic ties between our countries would be unnatural.

How would Soviet-Japanese rapprochement affect the United States? First, the scenario of a kind of Pacific *Rapallo* and Japan reorienting its foreign policy thinking are absolutely not viable. When Americans criticized the book by Shintaro Ishihara, *The Japan That Can Say No*, for mentioning such a possibility, both sides were bluffing. The level of interdependence makes drastic change in U.S.-Japanese relations nearly impossible. With rapid development of Soviet-American relations, the close link between the United States and Japan may even play a positive role for Soviet-Japanese normalization. In any case we will not link Soviet-Japanese relations and Japan's relations with third countries. All concerns that the Soviet Union will try to drive a wedge between Japan and the United States are groundless, especially in the context of improving Soviet-American relations.

As drastic changes in the structure of the triangle seem impossible, gradual adjustment to Japan's greater role in world affairs is up to the United States. Improvement in Soviet-Japanese relations cannot complicate this process.

Economically Soviet-Japanese rapprochement might have some positive effect on bilateral disputes between the United States and Japan in terms of diversification of Japan's exports, but it will be limited. The Soviet Union would not be able to absorb more than $10 to 15 billion of Japanese exports anyway, at least not in the foreseeable future.

In the regional context the improvement of Soviet-Japanese relations will undoubtedly decrease tensions in Northeast Asia and will affect our military posture in consistency with American interests. It may also have some positive effect on the solution of regional conflicts in Indochina and Korea.

Finally, how do we normalize relations with Japan? As we are deadlocked on the Kuriles, the Soviet side has put forth a proposal for the so-called third way of quiet, constructive dialogue and improvement in political, economic, and cultural relations. In the broader context of amelioration of the comprehensive situation in Asia and the Pacific and relaxation of military tensions in the region, the two sides to find a reasonable solution to the geographic issue. But as Alexander Yakovlev put it, you cannot climb a tree from the top.

A point about the Kuriles must be made. We have strong historical and legal arguments supporting our position. The Soviet Union did not violate international law. As we see the problem today, we are being asked to give up to Japan a part of our territory as a gesture of goodwill. Perestroika has moved far but not to the stage where we can give away our territory. We do not deny that a formula agreeable to both sides can be found. We are ready to talk, to discuss different aspects of a peace treaty and different aspects of our relations.

One should also not forget about the changes in the internal political situation inside the USSR. Five years ago our government could have any decision rubber stamped in the Supreme Soviet. Now the situation is quite different. Any unpopular proposal especially in such a sensitive area as territorial integrity simply will not be passed by the Soviet parliament.

The long history of relations between Russia and Japan and decades of cold war animosity left a number of problems in Soviet-Japanese relations. In order to resolve them the two sides should first take efforts to deepen trust and mutual understanding. The best way to achieve that is to develop friendly relations and establish broad ties in all fields. We hope President Gorbachev's visit to Japan in 1991 will become a turning point in this respect.

3

Prospects for
Improving Relations

Rajan Menon

Gorbachev, whether he succeeds or not, has worked so much magic and dashed so many of the axioms of Sovietology that occasionally I almost yearn, but only almost, for the days of Brezhnev, when it was much safer to predict and proclaim on matters Soviet. It is a much riskier business now.

Conversely, in the search for topics in which old patterns persist and the new has not been entirely vanquished by the old, one such topic is Japanese-Soviet relations, where the change has been far less dramatic compared with other areas of Soviet foreign policy, despite the fact that Foreign Minister Shevardnadze made two visits to Japan and President Gorbachev is about to make one. There have been innumerable Soviet proposals on arms control, trade, and economic cooperation.

But there has not been a fundamental transformation of the Japanese-Soviet relationship, nor is one likely. In short the atmosphere is better. The prospects are more hopeful. But that is it for the foreseeable future.

Why is this? What accounts for the relative immobilism in the relationship? Let me paint a portrait with broad strokes and offer six reasons for the immobilism.

First, there is a kind of perceptual rigidity of the relationship, where both sides continue to see each other if not as an antagonist, then as a party deserving of some suspicion. This is totally under-

13

standable in historical perspective. For most of this century the countries have been rivals in this region, and they have fought three wars. This perceptual rigidity is changing slowly, but very slowly.

Second, as the postwar legacy, the Soviets have seen Japan as a sort of platform for the projection of American conventional and nuclear power, and the Japanese in turn have seen the Soviet Union as the principal threat to their national security. Indeed, calling the Japanese quest for security in essence a quest for security from the Soviet Union is not too much of an exaggeration.

Third, the territorial problem not only is unresolved, but will be tough to resolve. In the Japanese case the Liberal Democratic party government has made this issue the litmus test for Japanese patriotism, resolve, and national honor. It has mobilized public opinion. It is supported by public opinion and by the broad spectrum of opposition parties. The government has painted itself into a corner where compromise or settling for half a loaf is difficult because the issue has been defined as one of such importance. Moreover, in the Japanese view compromise on their part at this juncture may not be advisable precisely because the combination of new thinking, flexibility, and the travails of the Soviet economy might bring forth a Soviet concession. The Japanese position may be to lie in wait and hope for an alteration of Moscow's position. This is not a realistic position.

From the Soviet point of view there have been some efforts, as witnessed in off-the-cuff interviews and scholarly articles, to debate the Northern Territories issue in the Soviet Union and even to explore some avenue for compromise. But the precondition for a compromise is a domestic political environment that is conducive for Gorbachev's making this kind of compromise. In that respect things are getting worse and worse. Mounting ethnic unrest calls into question Soviet territorial integrity for the first time since the 1940s. The economy is worsening. As Vasiliy Pospelov pointed out, public opinion is strong and the legislature is activated. The Northern Territories are militarily significant: together with the rest of the Kuriles, they fence in the Sea of Okhotsk, which is the basing point for Soviet strategic ballistic missile submarines. All of this makes a grand Soviet compromise not impossible but improbable. It would be surprising to see Gorbachev going to Japan in 1991, pulling a rabbit out of the hat, and trying to sweep the entire Northern Territories issue away by a fundamental compromise.

Fourth, the Soviets are over their early euphoria about the wonders that trade with Japan and Japanese investment can work. Their assessment is that even if the Northern Territories issue were to disappear, there would be a rather modest growth of Japanese trade and investment in the Soviet Union. The economic relationship is inhibited by a number of other things quite apart from the Northern Territories dispute. These obstacles are mounting instability in the Soviet Union, which makes Japanese investors nervous; the Japanese assessment that perestroika is at best uncertain; continuing Japanese unhappiness with various aspects of Soviet joint investment legislation, particularly provisions on taxation and on the repatriation of profits and hard currency; the difficulty of attracting and retaining quality labor in Siberia; and the opportunity costs of investing in the Soviet Union, given better markets such as existing ones in Southeast Asia, Korea, and Europe, and prospective ones such as Eastern Europe.

It is false to believe that if not for the Northern Territories, there would be a fundamentally different kind of Japanese-Soviet relationship, either politically or economically.

Fifth, the two countries continue to diverge on matters of security. The Soviet press, Soviet scholars in private discussions, Soviet academicians in journal articles, and Soviet leaders voice continuing and rather strident concern over the direction of Japanese security policy. They point to the rate of growth of the Japanese defense budget, which is far above that of NATO. They are not mollified when told that Japanese defense spending is just a hair above 1 percent of GNP. They point out that Japan's economy is the second largest in the world and that in absolute terms Japan's defense spending is one of the highest in the world. Furthermore the Japanese have demonstrated a rather awe-inspiring capacity in technology. Soviet military journals and discussions are replete these days with concern about the effect that the technological revolution of the late twentieth century could have on armaments, particularly in precision-guided munitions, deep-strike weapons, surveillance systems, and battle management techniques.

At least in the short run, the Soviet concern is not about the Japanese-Soviet bilateral military balance. Rather it is what Japan as

15

an ally of the United States can do to make American deployment options more flexible and diverse while lowering the costs. The Soviets are particularly concerned about the avenues that exist for cooperation between Japan and the United States in military technology. A 1983 agreement signed by Washington and Tokyo provides for this, and there is evidence that agreements being signed show that this is not, so to speak, merely a toothless document.

The Japanese assessment of the Soviet Union's military policy is also fairly hard-line. The Japanese are not persuaded that there has been a fundamental change in the nature of the Soviet threat. They do acknowledge that on the Sino-Soviet frontier there have been significant Soviet drawdowns. But in Primorsk, or the maritime province, the far eastern military district, that most critical for Japan, the Japanese Defense Agency's white paper points to continuing qualitative improvements and only a marginal quantitative diminution. In the security realm much still sets the countries apart.

Sixth, the Soviets have argued that their new policy toward Japan looks at Japan not as a function of the U.S.-Soviet relationship but as an independent, emerging center of power. If this policy is premised on the expectation of some form of Japanese Gaulism, the Soviets will be disappointed. Their own assessments now show that Japan continues to take its cues from the United States, whether it has to do with arms control negotiations with the Soviet Union or fundamental upgrading of the economic relationship or even political dialogue. Either the Japanese are fundamentally happy with the status quo and do not want a dramatically different relationship with the Soviet Union, or they are waiting and watching for what Washington does.

Finally, there is the hazardous business of prediction: I offer three. First, the Northern Territories issue is unlikely to be settled imminently. Certainly, theoretical solutions are possible. Joint administration is one possibility. A second possibility is the 1956 formula: the Hobomai Group and Shikotan, the two smallest and eastern islands, returned first, followed by Kunashiri and Etorofu, sandwiched by a peace treaty. A third possibility is development of economic and political relationships into a different kind of bilateral relationship, more conducive to compromise.

These are all theoretically possible. No evidence, based on discussions or research, indicates that any of these are imminent. Second, for all the Soviet alarm about Japan's growing defense capabilities, the Soviet Union may try to reduce and shape to its liking the U.S.-Japan military alignment. But it will not seek to rupture it, for the simple reason that the prospect of a Japan cut adrift from the United States means a Japan that might begin a quest for military self-sufficiency, which the Soviets certainly do not want.

The Soviets will ultimately come around to a solution, given appropriate security guarantees, for the same reasons they are likely to accept a united Germany anchored in NATO.

Third, there is no reason to expect a significant Japanese-Soviet economic rapprochement. The number of joint investment projects, the level of trade, and the scope of the joint investment projects are liable to remain small despite what might happen about the Northern Territories or the political relationship because of the numerous technical and economic factors fundamentally different between the two countries.

4

Japan Plays Follow the Leader

Masaru Tamamoto

When the question is asked, What will Japanese policy toward the Soviet Union be? I sense a certain skepticism about Japanese intentions. Will Japan cut some deal with the Soviet Union that may jeopardize American interests? Is it ready to do such a thing? The answer is clearly no.

Japan seeks no further advantages from the world and covets no benefits beyond what it already possesses. Clearly, Japan is concerned about what it should share of itself with the world more than worried about how to organize the world. Japan lacks political will, a crucial element in the making of a great power. And the United States remains the guarantor of Japan's willful, political innocence, an innocence that Japan has so carefully cultivated in the postwar era.

What is Japan's present and future policy toward the Soviet Union? A big debate is going on in Japan on how to deal with the Soviets. It is a debate that Japanese policy makers would prefer not to conduct. It is a debate that has been forced upon them by Mikhail Gorbachev and more important, by American responses to Gorbachev: Japanese leaders believe that a cool, distant, and minimum relationship with the Soviet Union is the best relationship possible. That things are changing, however, is recognized.

We do not know yet what conclusions the debate will produce, but one thing is certain. None of the participants in the debate—whether the office of the prime minister, the Foreign Ministry, the Defense Agency, even the opposition Socialist party, the ruling Liberal Democratic party, the major economic and industrial organi-

18

zations, or the media—advocates an independent Japanese foreign policy toward the Soviet Union or even a Japanese-led policy or Japanese-initiated policy for the U.S.-Japanese alliance.

The debate in Japan will remain inconclusive and will continue until the United States makes decisions about its Soviet policy in East Asia. And when the United States comes up with a Soviet policy, Japan will make decisions within the parameters set by the American leadership.

This is no different from what has been. Major strategic changes, political strategic changes for Japan have consistently followed the American lead. When Prime Minister Tanaka went to Moscow in 1973, it was only after Nixon and Brezhnev established their détente. The Japanese rapprochement with China followed the American lead. And this pattern has not changed. A thaw in Japanese-Soviet relations would characteristically follow a warming in U.S.-Soviet relations.

Today, there are no new policy initiatives between Japan and the Soviet Union. Why doesn't Japan have any new ideas about Soviet policy? One can get a sense of this from the Foreign Ministry. It is relatively easy to analyze Japanese relations with the Soviet Union because the principle of not separating economics and politics is strictly maintained. In most matters of foreign policy, a guiding principle is the separation of economics and politics. This exception for Soviet policy gives the Foreign Ministry the leadership in this matter. For other policies we witness competition between the Foreign Ministry and Ministry of International Trade and Investment, Ministry of Finance, and so on. But the Foreign Ministry role is clear in this because political considerations are paramount.

The Foreign Ministry maintains that the four islands must first be returned, then a peace treaty can be signed. Meanwhile discussions on economic issues can be conducted, but no substantive agreements can be reached until the islands are returned.

The issue of the four islands is ambiguous. It limits Japanese policy toward the Soviet Union. Territorial issues tend to become emotional and leave little room for compromise. Japan clearly wants the four islands back. But the issue is not that simple. It had been assumed that the Soviet Union would never give the islands back. As long as this issue is a precondition to a peace treaty, there was a sense of security that this minimum, cool, and distant relationship with the Soviet Union can be maintained. And with respect to Japanese thinking, this was the best policy.

Until the arrival of Gorbachev, little thought was given to what would happen if the islands were actually returned. And now the Foreign Ministry is searching for an answer. What kind of response is being formulated? Despite no clear answer there is a sense of what they are doing.

The Foreign Ministry has been releasing news to the Japanese press about recent meetings between the American secretary of state and the Soviet foreign minister. These releases reveal that the Hoppo Ryodo issue has been raised in a series of meetings conducted in the winter of 1989. The ministry seems to approve of this. And the position of the ministry seems to be that the issue should be settled within the context of the East-West framework, not between Japan and the Soviet Union alone. And if this is done, then Japan will have a clearer sense of how far it should go in improving relations with the Soviet Union.

By raising this issue with the United States, the Soviet Union understands that Japan is not going to move on its own: it has to involve the United States. John Foster Dulles remarked in the 1950s that the issue of the Northern Territories is much too important to leave to the Japanese, and so it remains.

There is no Japanese grand strategy toward the Soviet Union. The Defense Agency in its most recent white paper stressed that Soviet military capabilities in East Asia are increasing, that the situation in Asia is different from what is going on in Europe, and that the cold war has not ended in Asia. This is a rather extreme position. But unlike the recent trend in Europe, major uncertainty continues in the Korean Peninsula, Vietnam, Cambodia, and China. From Japan's perspective the world does not seem as safe as it does in the United States focus on the events in Europe. The end of the cold war will witness increased Japanese efforts to strengthen the U.S.-Japanese alliance, not to diminish it.

This brings us to the other major debate that is going on in Japan. This second debate is more important to Japan than the first. What will happen to the U.S.-Japanese security treaty, the fundamental pillar of Japan's foreign policy, if the Soviet Union is no longer America's enemy?

Great efforts are being made in Japan today to give new life to the security treaty even with a disappearing enemy. One result of such efforts is a greater emphasis on article 2 of the security treaty, which states that parties will seek to eliminate conflict in their international economic policies and will encourage economic collaboration between them. The tone of the debate tells us that the United States remains Japan's guide and protector in the world, and guarantor of Japan's willful political innocence.

This picture presented of Japan's lack of political will may seem counterintuitive to some. One may doubt that Japan can be so passive. A false connection may be made between Japan today and Japan of the militarist era, incidentally an anomaly in Japanese history. There may be doubt that Japan will be as peaceful as it has been for the past forty-five years. If there is doubt, it is only because of a lack of understanding of Japan's political and intellectual debates. Such a lack of understanding of the context gives unwarranted credence to men such as Shintaro Ishihara (the author of *The Japan That Can Say No*)—a marginal element of what mainstream Japanese are really thinking.

5

Japanese-American Security

William T. Pendley

In the context of the changing world environment, it is important to focus on the U.S.-Japanese security relationship. First and foremost, the relevance of the security relationship between the United States and Japan rests on mutually shared interests and the applicability of the security relationship to the world in the 1990s and beyond. The future applicability of that relationship cannot be intelligently discussed without looking at mutual interests. Those mutual interests must be better identified.

Despite the political, economic, and social changes, U.S. interests in Asia have remained fairly constant for most of this century:

1. the ability to provide for the protection of the United States, its interests, and its citizens
2. support for a regional balance in which no single nation can achieve domination in the region
3. freedom of the seas, which permits unconstrained flow of trade and commerce, as well as free access to markets and resources
4. support for democratic institutions and human rights

These have been fundamental interests. There is no reason why they would change. U.S. security policy has been driven to try to deter conflicts that would threaten these interests and to support those allies and friends who share those common interests.

Does Japan share these interests? With Japan as a producer and a processor economy, and its standard of living, even its economic survival rests more than most major nations on freedom of the seas and access to markets and resources.

Likewise Japan has recognized the need for regional balance and opposes the hegemony of any single nation in the region. It supports democratic institutions and human rights. These shared interests are at the core of the U.S.-Japan relationship. Additionally, Japan, like any sovereign nation, must provide for the protection of its land, its citizens and its interests.

As the second part of the consideration, why is there a security relationship? Why is that relationship with Japan unique? Is it necessary? The United States shares these mutual interests with a number of other nations with which we do not have a security relationship such as we have with Japan.

Our unique security relationship stems from a combination of internal and external restraints on Japanese military and security capabilities that result from the historical experience of Japan and the nations of the region, including the United States. Those restraints are not unilaterally imposed by nations other than Japan upon themselves. As a result of its historical experience in World War II, Japan has done so. The Japanese constitution limits Japan to self-defense forces. Its three non-nuclear principles prohibit Japan from possessing, introducing, and producing nuclear weapons. These self-imposed limitations are supported by the Japanese people. Significant internal debates still occur today as to whether in fact its self-defense, its current forces, do not exceed the self-defense provisions of the constitution.

The nations of the Asia Pacific region are sensitive to any increase in Japanese military capability. The experience of these nations, many occupied by the brutal Japanese military regime during World War II, produced a regional consensus against Japanese re-armament that cuts across differing political and economic systems. A Japan that would be militarily capable of pursuing objectives in support of Japanese interests, beyond a narrow definition of the defense of the Japanese home islands, is considered destabilizing by many nations in the region. Japan has been sensitive to those concerns of neighboring nations, and the Japanese people do not support and have not supported rearmament that would be destabilizing.

Nevertheless Japan has global economic and political power and vital security interests such as freedom of the seas and free access to resources and markets, which it must ensure.

What is the role of the U.S.-Japanese security relationship in a rapidly changing global environment? Is it still relevant? These questions are important because a security relationship with Japan is our most important bilateral alliance relationship. The answers to these questions are necessary to shape U.S. strategy in the Asia Pacific region as we move toward the twenty-first century. The role of the U.S.-Japanese security relationship will not change measurably but will provide three major elements of security: a nuclear deterrent for Japan in the absence of worldwide nuclear disarmament; deterrence and stability in Northeast Asia through the self-defense capability of Japan and the presence of U.S. forces with power projection capability; and U.S. forward deployed forces in the region to ensure freedom of the seas, access to resources and markets, and regional stability and balance.

Regarding the internal and external restraints on Japanese military capabilities, the major contribution of the United States to this security relationship should be the nuclear deterrent and the forward deployed military forces. Given the economic strength of Japan and the budget and deficit problems of the United States, Japan's major contribution to the security relationship should be the maintenance of a strong but not destabilizing self-defense force and economic support for U.S. forward deployed forces. With this shared approach to roles and missions within the security relationship, the United States and Japan can support their mutual interests as well as the broader interests of all nations for regional security and balance in Asia.

Still the question is asked time and time again: Is this relevant considering the changes taking place in the world today? The primary change in the world today is the balance between the Warsaw Pact and NATO or, more specifically, the bipolar balance between the United States and the Soviet Union. While that change fundamentally affects U.S. security relationships in Europe, it is far less significant in the Asia Pacific region.

The Soviet Union, before the collapse of her political and economic systems, was a political, economic, and military power in Europe. In the Asia Pacific region the Soviet Union has been only a military power, with limited political and economic influence, based almost exclusively on that military power.

In Europe regional security has hinged on bipolar balance. In Asia regional security has always been more complex, especially since the People's Republic of China became an independent actor in the arena and Japan became an economic superpower. A multipolar world emerged from the events of 1989 and 1990. Five of the six emerging major power centers in the world—the United States, Japan, China, India, and the Soviet Union—are located in the Asia Pacific region; they all have increasingly important political and economic and security interests.

In Asia there has never been a viable multilateral security structure like NATO—only a complicated web of bilateral relationships with the United States as the focal point. The U.S.-Japanese security relationship remains the most important element in maintaining regional stability and balance in the Asia Pacific region whether or not the Soviet Union remains a military power there. The security relationship has a far broader application than simply the deterrence of the Soviet Union, although that function remains essential as long as the Soviet Union maintains excessive military capability and power projection forces in Northeast Asia.

The Soviets are clearly interested in becoming players in the Asia Pacific region. There is a price, however, for that participation. That price is their demonstration that as a responsible partner the Soviet Union can contribute to regional balance and stability.

They can do that taking by a number of steps including signing a peace treaty and returning the Northern Territories, halting the transfer of armaments to destabilizing regimes such as North Korea, continuing its efforts to bring peace to Cambodia, and reducing its excessive power projection force structure in Northeast Asia.

These initiatives would be welcomed by both Japan and the United States and in turn might stimulate further U.S. force adjustments in the region. Such USSR actions would not, however, break the U.S.-Japanese security relationship, which supports the broader mutual interests of Japan and the United States in the region.

It is important that both Japan and the United States as well as other nations in the region have recognized that the bipolar balance between the United States and the Soviet Union, while significant for global and particularly European security reasons, is far different in

25

Asia. It has been a mistake in the past and would be a more serious mistake in the future to treat Asia in security affairs as a bipolar region. The nations of the Asia-Pacific region correctly recognize that independent of the relationship of the United States and the Soviet Union, or Japan and the Soviet Union, the U.S.-Japanese security relationship, coupled with U.S. forward presence, will remain critical to regional stability in Asia well into the twenty-first century.

It is important that as we consider this issue, we think about the security relationship in this broader context, although we are all hopeful for progress in Japanese-Soviet Union relationships.

6

Waiting for the Unlikely

Michael Powell

The renewed interest in Japanese-Soviet bilateral relationships evolves from a series of events and occurrences since Foreign Minister Shevardnadze's visit to Tokyo in 1986 when he tacitly acknowledged that a territorial dispute did exist. This was followed by the flurry of speeches by President Gorbachev at Vladivostok and Krasnoyarsk in which he set a much more conciliatory tone toward the region in general and Japan specifically, even referring to the Soviet relationship with Japan as vital.

Shevardnadze's visit in December 1988 set up a standing working group with the premise of addressing obstacles to a peace treaty between the two nations. Hope was raised of the possibility of Japanese-Soviet rapprochement.

Recently, however, many of these prospects have begun to dim. At the fourth meeting of the standing working group, Deputy Foreign Minister Rogachev returned to the traditional hard-line position that Japan relinquish its groundless claim on the border issues. Shevardnadze's March 1989 visit, a prelude to Gorbachev's visit in 1991, was cancelled in February 1989. And certainly the increasing difficulties and complexities of the territorial issues related to Lithuania and the Baltic states complicate the problem.

The problem is analogous to pieces of different puzzles piled on the ground for forty years. All of a sudden someone has flung these pieces into the air. With increased momentum and anticipation, we hope that miraculously they will land on the ground and neatly fit together as a beautiful picture of happy relations between the two nations.

But the most likely result is simply a new pile that is still mixed up. These pieces are not from the same picture and they are not likely to fit together without radical change.

The believers, those who believe in a bright future for Japanese-Soviet relations, point to the Soviet need for capital, technology, and Japanese-manufactured goods to help support a sagging economy; the increasing Japanese sense of isolation, fear of being swept away in the wake of the events of Eastern Europe and the internal changes in the Soviet Union; and the need for investment by the Soviet Union and the avarice of investing by the Japanese. All of these prospects are certainly alluring but much too simplistic and do not take into account their general incompatibility.

In international relations when any nation seeks to establish fertile relationships with another, it seeks to maximize or at least protect several key economic, security, political, and cultural and historical interests. Viewed from the Japanese perspective, little is to be gained by improved relationships with the Soviet Union. And one could argue that little might be gained by the Soviet Union from such a rapprochement.

Japanese society is a highly sophisticated economic power, a financial giant, and a leader in high technology. The nonconvertibility of Soviet currency and an economic infrastructure too starved to digest technologically rich Japanese manufactured goods make investment largely unattractive. Financiers recognize that credits and concessional loans currently granted will be written off as money lost without significant and dramatic reform of the Soviet economic infrastructure. Even the abundant natural resources of Siberia offer very little interest to a manufacturing culture increasingly reliant on high technology and one that has developed raw material markets elsewhere in the world.

Certainly from the security perspective, the U.S.-Japanese relationship will continue to be the one that the Japanese rely on for their security concerns. The Soviets had called for the abolition of the U.S.-Japanese security relationship as a necessary precondition to progress on the Northern Territories. But they later dropped that, for good reason. The security relationship is and will continue to be the underpinning of the entire U.S.-Japanese relationship. It is unlikely to change in the face of the post-traumatic cold war syndrome. The roles and missions that established the framework for the U.S.-Japanese security relationship contribute significantly to peace and stability and are politically sustainable in both countries. The mutual gains and benefits derived from this relationship are unlikely to be jeopardized in a Japanese attempt to move closer to Moscow.

Politically, Japan could significantly benefit from an improved relationship with the Soviet Union. Japan could certainly be increasingly concerned about being isolated as the lone Russia-basher in the shadow of the growing peace tree under which the rest of the world is basking. And the Japanese sense that they want to be recognized for the significant nation and important world player that they are. But their political interests ultimately are founded squarely in the West. The U.S.-Japanese global partnership best embodies the interests, the goals, the objectives, and the concerns of the Japanese people. In the foreseeable future the Japanese government is unlikely to stray from the umbrella of that partnership.

Certainly people have alluded to the cultural and historical difficulties of the past. Japanese public opinion polls continue to quantify the disdain and the distrust that many Japanese hold for the Soviet Union. Soviet statements often belittle and underestimate the potential of the Japanese and on occasion show little respect for them in some of their dealings.

Even if the relationship were to become warmer, it could never become a loving one. From the Soviet perspective it is unclear whether any tangible benefits are to be gained. Certainly the problems in Lithuania severely complicate the problems resolving contested property and territorial issues stemming from the Yalta Conference.

From the Soviet perspective the Northern Territories are Mother Russia. They are not a province. They are not a region embedded within the union. They are considered Soviet territory and therefore represent a much more complicated situation than that of states like Lithuania.

The Soviet Union cannot help but be concerned that giving up the Northern Territories unconditionally, which is insisted on by the Japanese, is to give away the only powerful card in their hand. And it is unlikely to happen without some serious concessions or compromises on the part of Japan. Certainly a warmer relationship would not do anything to undercut the U.S. military commitment to the region and the U.S. commitment to its relationship with Japan.

From a detached view one can begin to understand the actions taken by both countries. Japan continues to maintain rigorously its staunch position on the Hoppo Ryodo on the basis of principle more than the strategic value of those islands. That is easy to do. It is easy to take the high ground when little if anything is to be gained by compromise. And thus the two sides are increasingly unlikely to give way on their positions.

Recently, murmurs were heard in Japan. A Diet member, Shin Kanemaru, speculated on the possibility of returning two islands followed by unspecified negotiations on the remaining two—a comment greeted by an uproar from the Liberal Democratic party. Kanemaru even had to issue somewhat of an apology for his statements. But what is seen in Japan is often just academic speculation, consideration, political power plays, and factional politics. It is good public relations to see Gorbachev. It is good public relations politically to find a creative solution to the Northern Territories. But remarks about such proposals are targeted for the Japanese political audience.

The Soviet Union seems increasingly to be pursuing a policy to isolate Japan further in the international scene, to coax the United States to recognize that Japan is not quite a member of the superpower club. When the issue of the Northern Territories was raised at the December 1989 summit at sea between the United States and the Soviet Union, the Soviet Union almost replied, "Well, we'll let the Japanese know you raised it; we know they put you up to it, and it's not really a concern," in an attempt to separate the United States from that issue.

What does normalizing the relationship mean? Does it mean much more than they already have? Both nations maintain embassies in each other's countries. They continue, with the exception of Gorbachev, to exchange high level visitors and to pursue quite a rigorous diplomatic agenda. What more of substance can be gained, given the incongruence of each other's self-interests, seems quite questionable. If we are waiting for full-fledged rapprochement between the Soviet Union and Japan, clearly we are waiting for the unlikely.

30

7

The Asian Connection

Thomas W. Robinson

Three issues are at the base of contemporary Japanese-Soviet relations. The first, and perhaps the most important, is the domestic revolution in the Soviet Union led by President Mikhail Gorbachev under the two slogans of glasnost and perestroika. This carries three implications that bear directly on the Soviet approach to Japan. First, U.S.-Soviet relations have changed fundamentally, particularly in the military-strategic arena. Second, Soviet policy in Asia has also changed for the better. The Russians are no longer the same military threat in that region because Moscow's internal situation will not allow for such a policy. That is true despite the lack of a general drawdown in Soviet forces in Asia. Third, as a result the Kremlin has decided to improve its ties with Japan by facing up to the need to negotiate with Tokyo over the return of the four Northern Islands seized at the end of World War II.

The second issue is scarcely less important. U.S.-Japanese relations are in flux for the first time since 1945. Trade differences dominate the headlines, the product of different economic fundamentals: comparative land size, resource availability within national boundaries, socio-cultural-linguistic factors, population densities, and the like. These variables constrain two fully developed economies with industrious, educated work forces to compete (as they should) for world markets, each on the basis of its comparative advantages. The problem is that the Americans perceive some built-in, but still artificial, advantages for Japan that must be corrected, while the Japanese see themselves as a people still (after nearly a century and

31

a half) under stress from the outer world that constrains them to protect their society and their economy from what could in their eyes once again become overwhelming.

These differing evaluations of the bilateral relationship are negatively affecting the domestic political situation in the two countries. This could well spill over into the security realm, as Americans call for an evening up of the defense burden and as the Japanese, perhaps too eagerly, agree and go onto provide themselves with a large, modern military force that could project Japanese military power throughout Asia and perhaps the globe. These trade problems have not yet affected the security tie between Japan and the United States, but they might become a central disturbing element.

The third issue is the change in the very nature of the international economy and of security assistance. We live in a world that is highly interdependent, in which domestic economic systems are configured by trade relationships and by rapid economic development in some areas. In Asia a number of new military powers have emerged while in Europe the security equation has been transformed.

The internal situations in Japan or the United States could well change; Donald Hellmann could probably talk a great deal about that. And that change could influence the relations between the Russians and the Americans and the Japanese. But the consideration at hand is the triangular relationship of these three countries. First, is there is such a triangle? I am not sure of this. If one looks at the military strategic relationship, such a triangle is not worth talking about much. Japan is after all still not an independent variable. It does not have the kinds and amounts of force that count, although it could procure them. Only because we are asked to talk about the future do we bother to talk about the military strategic equation and include Japan in it at all.

It is not worth talking about a triangle regarding probabilities of Japanese-Soviet rapprochement at American expense. That is not in the cards for reasons that have been already presented in this analysis. It is also not relevant since the Russians cannot effectively insert themselves between the Americans and the Japanese. The Soviet Union does not have the economic or diplomatic marbles to play in that game and will not have them soon. And it is unlikely that Soviet diplomatic maneuverings will be able to make up for the lack of those policy instruments with the exception of the military.

Conversely it pays to talk about this triangle in the sense of a major improvement in Japanese-Soviet relations and a major breakdown in Japanese-U.S. relationships. The latter is not impossible in both the security and the economic spheres. That would transform the trans-Pacific and would form the basis of a new world political situation. That seems highly unlikely today, but if one looks at trends, one ought at least to begin to consider that negative scenario. It also makes sense to talk about the triangle in a positive sense. A major improvement in Japanese-Soviet relations, in the context of today's major improvement in Soviet-U.S. ties, and a serious future decline in Japanese-American relations would also be a major departure in Asian global affairs.

What are American interests in seeing to, or opposing changing and presumably improving the Japanese-Soviet relationship? First, we may be confronted with a China that is increasingly strong and unfriendly to the United States, with a relatively weak, a perhaps post-perestroika Soviet Union, and still a Japan that is growing, rearming slowly, and separating itself from the United States. That could precipitate a new relationship in Asia, particularly one of renewed closeness between the Russians and the Chinese. That could only be highly detrimental to the United States.

Conversely a Japanese-Soviet rapprochement godfathered by the United States could reassure Moscow and give it reason in Asia not to stand with the Chinese in a renewed hard-line alliance against the United States. That is one good reason for fostering improvement in Japanese-Soviet relations.

The second reason is that in the incipient transformation of the structure of Asian international relations, with a rise to superpower status in every regard for both Japan and China, the rise to great power status of India, and probably a reunited Korea, the American interest is to have in Asia as many and as strong a set of players as one can find. That is reason enough to keep the Soviet Union in Asia as a major player. It is also good reason to have ties everywhere in Asia, to construct a system without a built-in tendency to break down into competing alliances and alignments.

In this situation, which is the direction in which Asia is tending, improved Japanese-Soviet relations are a good thing for the United States. How can Japanese-Soviet relations be improved in a manner that still remains favorable to the United States? First of all, some

33

things will not do. A mere return of the four Northern Islands as the sole condition for improvement in Japanese-Soviet relations will not occur. That is totally unrealistic. There are too many problems for that in Soviet internal affairs and for Soviet relations with its neighbors.

Conversely, it also will not do to put the Hoppo Ryodo issue aside, much as the Americans and the Chinese put aside the Taiwan question in 1972. Japanese internal politics will not allow for that, nor will Japanese attitudes toward the Soviet Union.

If it is proper and desirable to break the impasse between Japan and the USSR, how can it be accomplished? The only way is to imbed the resolution of the Northern Territories dispute in some larger agreement, one that would include changes in the American relationship with the two countries involved. What elements would go in that package deal?

Some have already been mentioned. One element would be an agreement that the Japanese invest much more heavily in the Soviet Union and trade much more with Moscow. In return the Kremlin would hand back some, if not all, of the Northern Territories. Parenthetically, it is not written in stone that the Japanese require the return of all of those islands. They say so, but once negotiations begin and the Soviet Union tempts them with a series of economic concessions and other elements, the Japanese might settle for three of the four islands.

The second component is joint administration of the Northern Islands for a period, after which they revert to Japan. Third, a package could include one or a series of arms control agreements between the Americans and the Russians in Northeast Asia. One could write its terms however one would like. On the American side aspects could include the Misawa Air Base, the ballistic missile submarines, the carrier task forces, and the maritime strategy. One would have to include a Japanese commitment not to rearm, at least not heavily. On the Soviet side would be concern about Backfires, Blackjacks, nuclear submarines, regionally targeted Soviet missiles, and high-performance jet aircraft.

A fourth element in that package would be possible joint U.S.-Japanese investment in Siberia, traded off on the Soviet side by opening up Vladivostok and Nakodka as a joint export processing zone and probably the emergence of a special convertible Soviet ruble in the Far East. Finally, this should be developed in the context of the emerging American interest in cooperation with the Soviet Union in Asia.

The case for U.S.-Soviet cooperation in Asia now exists. It is a strong case germane to Japanese-Soviet rapprochement. The case rests on the relative weakness of both superpowers in Asia: the Soviets, out of their domestic situation and their difficulty even of accessing Asia; the Americans, out of their success in fostering the development and growth and power of indigenous Asian powers aligned with the United States (the best example being Japan).

The second reason is the fluid nature of the Asian security and economic systems regarding both Japan and China, as Korea, Thailand, Indonesia, certainly India, and possibly even Viet Nam emerge as middle powers in their own rights. Third is the remaining work for Washington and Moscow in that region regarding the remnants of the cold war, such as the question of arms control in Northeast Asia.

Last are the threats to peace in Asia that stem from North Korea, the Taiwan-mainland China situation, the expansion of raw Chinese power in the region, the Philippine situation, Cambodia, and Kashmir, to name a few. The Americans and the Russians ought to be dealing jointly with these threats.

Together the United States and the Soviet Union can help Asia transit to a different systemic organization, a form in which Japan and its resurgent power can be a force for peace that is acceptable to all. But if the Americans and the Russians remain at odds in Asia, the region will become a free-for-all arena, where the prospects for conflict are high and Japan's role less responsible and acceptable than over the past several decades.

The Japanese, Russians, and Americans all have much to do in Asia. Working together, the prospects for peace, democracy, and modernization are high. If we do not seize this opportunity, if we let matters drift, the prospects for conflict, for suppression of popular desires, and for the drift downward to backwardness will also be high.

8

The Alaska Solution

Donald C. Hellmann

The newfound interest in Japanese-Soviet relations is breathtaking, particularly at this juncture. Even more astonishing is the general tenor of this volume: basically no one wants to change the status quo much. That is an accurate assessment from the perspective of policy makers in Washington. But Washington is a kind of subculture in the United States. This volume would be unnecessary if policy makers were in control.

Events are forcing decisions. What are these events? Thomas Robinson touched on some of them. These events are forcing four major issues.

First, the whole notion of Japanese-Soviet bilateral relations is seen from an economic, strategic and territorial point of view. First of all, the territorial issue—which this volume assumes to be solved, so that relations between the two countries can be considered—is a terribly interesting one. The Japanese have long maintained, namely, since August 1956, when the Foreign Ministry issued a statement to that effect, that they owned all of the islands legally. Prime Minister Yoshida's Diet proceedings on the San Francisco Peace Treaty show that Japan did not have legal claim to them. Their legal claim to the islands is ambiguous. And I would agree with Vasiliy Pospelov that the Soviet legal claim to Etorofu and Kunashiri is defensible. Historically the Japanese may be correct, but legally the issue is moot and it is not likely to be resolved easily.

Second, the resolution of the territorial dispute is not a legal issue. A deal will be cut involving all kinds of things.

One solution—different from Vasiliy Pospelov's—is what I call the Alaskan solution. A century ago, we bought, they sold us Alaska for $7 million. Likewise a monetary value could be put on those little islands. Japan is now assessed at five times the value of the United States. One could take the per square foot value of Japan, project it on those islands and establish a price. Mikhail Gorbachev would then have more hard currency than he could get with years of negotiating with Deutschebank. Such a real estate deal may or may not be a possibility, but if the Russians do not explore it or explore some version of that, they are surely do not understand capitalist and entrepreneurial ways.

A third point, the idea that the Japanese and the Russians understand one another well enough to initiate bilateral contacts, is absurd. Soviet lack of understanding of Japan and how to manipulate the Japanese system rivals our own. The Japanese capacity to deal with the Soviet Union is equally appalling. Until recently Soviet studies in Japan were nonexistent. One small place in Hokkaido deals with this issue. It has suddenly become fashionable to study the Soviet Union. But by any standard the Japanese are institutionally and personally incapable of dealing easily with these kinds of issues with the Soviet Union, certainly in a geopolitical sense. They know it, and they are unlikely to take any initiatives in this regard.

What about economic relations between the two countries? First of all, the Japanese will get involved in Siberia and the rest of the Soviet Union not because there are good deals there. There are some, but they are marginal, and the risks are substantial. That is a major reason why Japanese corporations have not been involved. They have looked at the economics and decided the risk was not worthwhile.

The Japanese will be involved because others are. Hyundai just signed an agreement to build a naphtha cracking plant in western Siberia; this will involve billions of dollars. No Japanese prime minister or industrialist would allow the Koreans or anyone else a dominant position in the development of Siberia. The incentives for Japanese investment will not come from technological considerations or even from what the Soviet Union says but rather from the economic initiatives that other Asian and European countries and even the United States may undertake.

An interesting economic issue rises. Until now Japan's trade with the Soviet Union has been out of balance. Until the early 1980s

Japan's economic involvement in the Soviet Union was almost solely in the development of Siberia. Ninety percent of Soviet imports from Japan were heavy machinery and equipment related to the developments in Siberia. This has changed somewhat in the past few years, and how far it will change depends on the Soviet economic revolution because developing Siberia is a relatively low priority when compared with restructuring the whole society.

Japan's role if it expands will not be limited to Siberian development but rather will encompass the broader goals of Soviet economic restructuring. Moreover that focus is more a function of what the Soviet Union chooses and less of what Japan wants.

Security is in many ways the most interesting and complex relationship. Not only do the Japanese and the Soviets not understand each other, they do not like each other. Japanese school textbooks, for example, depict the Soviet Union unfavorably at best. It is unlikely that this attitude is going to change into a groundswell of affection. Nevertheless policy is not made that way. If a deal is to be cut, a deal will cut. The public will be dragged along, just as Japanese consumers have been dragged along, behind economic policy.

Should Japan and the Soviet Union alter or can they alter the U.S.-Japan security arrangement? Ever since they started writing defense white papers, back in the 1970s, the Japanese have justified their defense budget in terms of the Soviet threat. No wonder they want the cold war to continue in Asia. If virtually the entire Pentagon budget were dependent on one single issue and published annually to justify that, the Pentagon would try to square the circle and keep it in place as a matter or survival.

The U.S.-Japanese security relationship is an interesting one. The Russians accuse the Japanese and the Americans of an imperial alliance, when in fact the Russians are relieved by this alliance. A breakdown of U.S.-Japanese relations over trade or anything else would create, at the least, an unknown: a Japan not necessarily remilitarizing but an unknown—a loose cannon, something out of control. And that is the last thing the Soviet Union wants.

There is room for Soviet-U.S. cooperation in Asia.

I was in the Soviet Union a few years ago. After several glasses of vodka, one of the Russian academicians proposed a policy toward Japan that I now refer to as the shut-up policy. He suggested that if the Japanese in any way try to interfere with preserving the status quo, Washington and Moscow should together tell them to shut up.

The Japan-U.S. security relationship is to our benefit, as has been admirably pointed out by several in this volume, even the Soviet diplomat. Why should it change? Because the structure of the international system has changed, the meaning of security has changed, the purpose for deployment of forces has changed. Anyone listening to Congress or listening to the budget discussions in the Pentagon knows that.

The Japanese do not share our democratic values. Although unfashionable, on this issue I side with Richard Nixon, who said essentially that if anyone thinks the Japanese would encourage the Chinese to be democratic, he is smoking pot. The Japanese-U.S. alliance does not mean promoting democracy the way we understand it, either in Europe or in China. This is a complex topic to be saved for another discussion.

A new international division of labor is in order. The Japanese-U.S. alliance cannot continue in its present form, not just because the Russians may have changed their spots or are undergoing upheaval. It is so asymmetrical in terms of international realities, economic and military, that it cannot continue in its current form. That a continuation of this alliance is good, that the United States should bear, as they have in the past, the responsibility for maintaining order in the Western Pacific and negotiating both strategic and conventional arms control with the Soviet Union is hard to dispute. Shortly after President Bush came into office he met with then Prime Minister Takeshita. The communique they issued called for a new international division of labor in which we would maintain order and they would give aid. Former Secretaries of State Vance and Kissinger seconded this, and the chorus was loud and resonant.

This is an absurd suggestion: that we maintain order and the Japanese assume the role of Santa Claus distributing goodies to the third world. Three-year-olds playing in a sandbox would not make a deal like that; that is, let's play cops and robbers—you be the good guy all the time and I will be the bad guy. Yet we made the deal.

This bespeaks a recognition at the highest level in Washington that change in the world order must occur. It is also indicative of the poverty of solutions to what that change might be.

A fundamental change is in order in the security relations

between the three countries in the Western Pacific under discussion. There are many venues for doing this. One is to redefine internationalization of the sea lanes in the region, a process in which the Russians probably could be involved, with constabulary security as the replacement for containment. Only the United States is in a position to take such initiatives. And that is why many agree that Japanese-Soviet relations in the end will ultimately improve only by initiatives that come from Washington.

9

Japan's High Principle

Richard N. Perle

There is an old story about the French, Russian, and Japanese businessmen who formed a company in Central Africa; the profitability depended on the success with which they violated the customs regulations of the country. In due course they were caught smuggling and as justice is swift there, sentenced to be executed. The morning of the execution came. The young officer in charge of the firing squad offered each a last wish. He turned first to the Frenchman. The Frenchman said, "I will sing while the band plays the 'Marseillaise,' please." He turned next to the Japanese. The Japanese said, "I would like to deliver a short lecture on the Northern Territories and the international law pertaining to their legitimate possession." The officer turned last to the Russian. The Russian said, "Just shoot me second: I don't want to hear that lecture again."

Vasiliy Pospelov says that perestroika has not yet moved so far as to give up Soviet territory. Perestroika has not moved very far at all if recent decisions regarding restructuring of the Soviet economy are any indication. But precisely because perestroika has not yet moved very far, in the long run the Soviet Union will indeed give up this territory.

The failure of the Soviet economic system and the collapse of the Soviet empire will in due course lead to the Soviet Union relinquishing its hold over the Northern Territories. The British gave up their empire, the French gave up their empire, in neither case cheerfully or willingly, in one case rather more peacefully than the other. But we are seeing the end of imperialism in the modern world.

41

In due course this will include the Northern Territories as well. Not even James Baker and Hans-Dietrich Genscher can stop this process in Europe, and nobody will stop it in the Pacific either.

Rajan Menon has said that the Liberal Democratic party has painted itself into a corner on the issue of the Northern Territories. That seems a bit like observing Michelangelo on the scaffolding of the Sistine Chapel and saying that he is painting himself into a corner. But oh what a corner! The intractability, the intransigence, the stubbornness, the high principle with which a succession of Japanese administrations has viewed the issue of the territories will turn out to be the right policy because eventually those territories will be returned. There is nothing wrong with a little stubbornness in a good cause.

Michael Powell said that if the Soviets return the territories, they will give up the only powerful card in their hand. But one must question the usefulness of that card. It has, among other things, prevented the development of a constructive relationship between Japan and the Soviet Union for rather a long time. On reflection it has not clearly proved to be an asset for the Soviet Union.

Michael Powell also observed that it is easy to take the high ground. But if anybody has been observing President Bush's handling of the Lithuanian situation, he might come to the conclusion that it is hard to take the high ground.

Thomas Robinson has hopes for arms control in Northeast Asia. It is hard to imagine how one could develop a significant arms control solution in Northeast Asia when current arms control negotiations are most likely to have the effect of shifting the center of gravity of Soviet military power from Europe toward Asia. Unless significant Soviet forces are to be eliminated entirely, the situation may actually become somewhat worse in Asia rather than better.

Finally, it is hard to believe Donald Hellmann that Japanese investment decisions will be made not on the basis of rational calculation as to potential profits but simply in an imitative mode to invest because others are investing. The Japanese are rather shrewd and successful investors. One would look a long time before finding the Japanese investing for silly reasons like that one.

And it is a bit unfair to say that the Japanese Defense Agency, in its white papers, is misconstruing the security situation that Japan has faced, or that it wishes to continue the cold war in Asia. One could forgive the Japanese Defense Agency for examining Soviet military forces in the Pacific in relation to, say, Japanese military forces in the Pacific, which certainly do not pose a threat to the Soviet Union, and concluding that it is right to be concerned about its own security.

And finally, it is doubtful that the Soviets do not desire a breach between the United States and Japan. They have gone to some considerable lengths on many occasions precisely to precipitate difficulties in the U.S.-Japanese relationship. And these fashionable theories that the Soviets really want a unified Germany in NATO and that they really want a solid U.S.-Japanese alliance are rubbish in both cases.

10

Hope for the Future

A Discussion

RAJAN MENON: I agree with Richard Perle's analogy of the Sistine Chapel. But the Liberal Democratic party would find it difficult to concede on the Hoppo Ryodo even if it wanted. I agree that the Japanese do not want to and probably will not.

The Soviets have made mischief in the past. But to the extent that the Soviets think there are changes in Japanese defense policy and given that a Japan cut adrift would at the least create uncertainties, one must reexamine the axiom that the Soviets would like to see some aspects of the security alliance changed. I stand by my point: severing that relationship would not be in the interest of the Soviet Union.

About whether the Soviets will accept a united Germany as part of NATO, I do not know whether it is rubbish or not. Richard Perle is confident that it is. We shall see.

MASARU TAMAMOTO: There are several reasons for Japanese investments in the Soviet Union. Agreed, it does not seem profitable for most companies. But if it happens, it will be politically motivated: the government will decide on some positive move. And the government will have to guarantee those investments. Some businesses will go in kicking and screaming even with some sort of insurance. That is probably how business investments would happen.

WILLIAM PENDLEY: I particularly agree with the idea that stressing the triangles is misleading, although it is fashionable to do these

44

days. When one travels to Japan, allusions to triangles are made all the time—whether the U.S.-China-Japan triangle, a U.S.-Soviet-and some-other triangle. But in Asia a triangle oversimplifies the issue because there are always many more sides than three.

I was a bit upset to hear the discussion in terms of arms control, focusing again as if this is a bipolar region and Soviet-U.S. arms control is what we seek. That would be a tragic mistake, given that it is not a bipolar region.

MICHAEL POWELL: There are trends and there are possibilities for significant improvement in Japanese-Soviet relations. But trends ultimately will be more symbolic than substantive, and little can take place that will significantly change the balance of world affairs or the actual relationship.

Certainly there is potential for cultural exchange, confidence-building measures, various other agreements, even a peace treaty. But fundamentally the nature of the existing relationship will not change substantively.

VASILIY POSPELOV: I cannot agree that the Soviet Union and Japan will gain little from normalization of their relations. We could similarly ask ourselves, What do we gain from the end of the cold war? What do we gain from the normalization of Soviet-U.S. relations? New, friendly relations will bring fruits to the people of the USSR and Japan as well as to other countries.

In regard to the proposal to sell the islands, let me say the following: recently *Pravda* commented on a letter from a reader in the Far East. The author said that for twenty years the USSR had sold its natural resources for hard currency, and now this hard currency has been wasted. Neither natural resources nor territory can be recovered said the reader, and selling them is not a proper way to deal with our economic problems. Public opinion is clearly against this idea.

With regard to arms control, nobody denies that the situation in the Pacific is multipolar. There are different threats and different sources of danger. Let us first make certain moves that do not affect the capability to respond to other threats. We may start not with the arms reductions but with confidence-building measures. Second, let us address the bilateral concerns of the Soviet Union, and America,

45

in Northeast Asia. I do not see why we should not discuss such things.

THOMAS ROBINSON: The relationship between America, Japan, and the Soviet Union cannot be seen by itself out of context. It must be embedded in broader trends and broader developments. These include trends in Asia and the strategic triangle. The Chinese are an important, disturbing variable. And one must consider what is happening in Europe.

Richard Perle is absolutely right. If arms control agreements in Asia take the form that we see them taking in Europe, they could well lead to a repositioning of Soviet forces presently in Europe to a concentration in the Asian portions of the Soviet Union unless the forces were disbanded altogether.

We had better bring in the Asian component to the European strategic arms control relationship. We cannot keep it under the table; it cannot be hidden there anymore. It is counterproductive to have an arms control agreement in one area of the world if it affects the situation detrimentally in another.

DONALD HELLMANN: Masaru Tamamoto responded adequately to Richard Perle's question about investments. That is the way the Japanese operate.

His theory about controlled collapse of empire is an interesting one. It factors out policy initiatives and says presumptively the collapse will occur as we all watch. I hope he is right.

Does Eastern Europe share the comparable legal status of the Northern Territories? That merits further inspection.

The end of the cold war—which is not over yet—has seen a rebirth of nationalism, not just in an international sense but in the sense of protectionism. We cannot really talk about Japanese, Soviet, and U.S. relations even in a broad context without addressing the question of defining national interests in a new way. And this goes beyond just deployment of forces or weapons, counting a host of issues, many of them economic, some of them territorial, and most assuredly institutional arrangements such as alliances and multilateral pacts. That is where I would like to see the emphasis in future discussion.

46

QUESTION: How can the Russians justify taking the Northern Islands and never returning them? Even the Americans, who contributed more to winning the war in the Pacific eventually returned Okinawa to the Japanese.

VASILIY POSPELOV: It is not a useful exercise to go into history and count whose contribution in the war was greater. It was simply a different kind of war from the Soviet perspective. The Soviet Union fought 1 million Japanese—the famed Kwantung army—in Korea and Manchuria.

In terms of the Northern Territories our position is based on the Yalta Agreement, and the United States was party to it. Some analysts, as reported in the Soviet press, say that maybe from the U.S. side, it was a deliberate oversight in San Francisco that the treaty did not define properly the fate of these territories. Initially, just after World War II, the USSR and the United States did not differ on this issue. Obviously the United States later changed its position for certain political reasons.

Another element of our principal position is that this is a bilateral problem with Japan and internationalization will not contribute to the solution. I will refrain from further comments on the territorial issue.

DONALD HELLMANN: There is in the legal sense a distinction between Etorofu and Kunashiri, the two big northern islands and Habomai and Shikotan, the smaller islands. They were addressed in the San Francisco treaty in the same category as Okinawa.

The question about the reversion of Okinawa is a legitimate one. The phrase used in the San Francisco conference essentially says that the territorial right to these islands would be settled by a subsequent international conference at a future unspecified time. Habomai and Shikotan, which are much smaller, were part of the prefecture of Hokkaido in prewar Japan. In 1956 the Soviet Union agreed to revert them in exchange for a security treaty. In purely legal terms that offer is probably fair.

The ownership of Etorofu and Kunashiri can be disputed historically and is legitimately done so. But in a legal sense the issue is ambiguous. The issue will probably not be resolved definitively. And if they are not sold like Alaska, some other fig leaf will be found to

47

allow money to change hands in the interest of putting the issue to rest.

QUESTION: Mr. Tamamoto said that the relationship with the Soviet Union was less important to Japan than its relationship with the United States. He said that the Japanese government was comfortable with this situation, and if there were to be any change at all, it would follow the U.S. lead. Would developments that do not involve the Soviet Union, such as economic tensions between the United States and Japan and poor performance in the Western Pacific, change the Japanese outlook on the Soviet Union?

MASARU TAMAMOTO: This is highly unlikely. Japan's relations with the United States are too important. It will not happen.

DONALD HELLMANN: There is not much discussion of this issue in Japan. Yet it is serious, and there should be more consideration of this in the United States. As pointed out, U.S. action, to a large extent, would bring about change. We should be concerned about this because what the United States does as far as its Asian policy, exclusive of the economic interface, is critical to the Japanese-U.S. relationship.

QUESTION: I was surprised to hear Mr. Powell say that Mikhail Gorbachev's speeches in Vladivostok and Krasnoyarsk were conciliatory and that he conceded the importance of the USSR's participation in Asia. Most of us remember those speeches as expansionist.

MICHAEL POWELL: The speeches both in Vladivostok and Krasnoyarsk were at a minimum the symbolic recognition of the importance of the region, which we had not seen diplomatically in quite some time. There was a great deal of reading between the lines. Flexibility was implied where before there was no flexibility. We saw a potential departure from what had long been a clearly articulated, rigid position to at least an offer of some room for change.

Prior to that, the Soviets left absolutely no room for interpretation of what they meant. And those speeches began to offer, at least to specialists in the area, the possibility and the flexibility in the language to consider the possibility of significant change. Certainly in the Krasnoyarsk speech actual references to Japan as vital, to use Gorbachev's word, are the beginning of an evolution of change in the policy for the region.

THOMAS ROBINSON: In some respects too much attention has been given to the Vladivostok speech, although it surely was a departure from previous stands and a positive initiative. No one disagrees with that.

As Michael Powell was saying, that speech did reverse what was a longstanding Soviet policy of playing a zero sum game in Asia by trying to break out of that mold. Indeed it was reflected in personnel changes in various reaches of the Soviet Foreign Ministry, replacing a group of people who had an inflexible orientation with others who were much more positive.

It was also an initiative toward China. The improving situation we find in Sino-Soviet relations today is the product of that initiative, although there are precursors, such as the Leonid Brezhnev speech of October 1982.

It also was an attempt by the Russians to indicate continued interest in Asia. That is important and must be recognized by the rest of the world, not just Europe. The idea was to balance a new Soviet policy toward Europe with a Soviet policy in Asia. Soviet initiatives under Gorbachev toward Europe and the United States are almost always followed by (or almost coterminal in some cases) with a positive departure toward Asia. The Vladivostok speech is an example.

Most important, it was an admission by the Russians that their policy toward Asia failed and that they are going to try to turn it around. It was an admission that failed policy was based too much on the military instrument of power. If the Soviets are to become part of Asia, they must exercise other instruments of policy, particularly economic. Therefore an invitation was offered to Asia to help the Russians acquire this kind of economic power and become part of Asia in the real sense of the term.

VASILIY POSPELOV: The Vladivostok speech, the *Merdeka* newspaper interview, then the Krasnoyarsk speech were focused on the definition of new Soviet policy in Asia. By no means can it be characterized as expansionist.

In the *Merdeka* interview Gorbachev accepted the double-zero concept, that is, zero intermediate-range missiles for Europe and zero for Soviet Asia. It paved the way to the signing of the INF Treaty between the Soviet Union and the United States.

Significant parts of these speeches were devoted to our bilateral relations with the Pacific countries. After that, during the past two or three years, we have seen real breakthroughs in bilateral relations with many countries, not only with China, where normalization of relations is a clear result of the changing Soviet attitude, but also with South Korea, Australia, and ASEAN countries. The changes in our military posture, although they are doubted sometimes, are real. They are also a result of reassessment of the issue, which started in 1986 with the Vladivostok speech.

QUESTION: Mr. Robinson said that if we do not seize the opportunity to work together in Asia, the prospects for suppression and backwardness in the region are high. Is it too late to prevent a new Sino-Soviet alliance directed against the United States? After all, the United States could do little by way of fostering Japanese-Soviet rapprochement to offset potential benefits to the Soviet Union of Soviet-Chinese cooperation.

THOMAS ROBINSON: Things are never too late. In some cases diplomacy may be late but not in this case. The Li Peng visit to Moscow is another step toward improvement in Soviet-Chinese relations. More steps are yet to come.

But there are inherent limitations to that improvement, given the nature of the situation between China and the USSR, their histories, and the attitudes that the two peoples have toward each other.

We have to worry about the possibility of a rapprochement between the Soviets and Chinese that is directed against the United States and indeed Japan. It could come because of forces beyond our control, such as a change in Soviet leadership.

But my point is a different one. I am looking at the long term and trying to assess the security changes in the Asian arena and more broadly in the global system. When we look at those, we see the emergence—whether slower or more rapidly—of a strong, power-projectionist China and a Japan that in the long run will have its own large military force in all probability. And it does not necessarily have to evolve despite the United States or as a result of a break with the United States.

If in the past Asia was like Europe, bifurcated between Soviet and American camps—with the possible exception of China, which tended to move between the two for its own security—and if we are replacing that with a multipolar Asia, it follows that a Soviet Union that is more friendly toward Japan makes sense.

JO DEE JACOB: In conclusion, the time is right for the Soviets, Japanese, and Americans to go beyond the Hoppo Ryodo and talk seriously about normalization of relations in Northeast Asia. Cautious optimism for resolution of the territorial dispute and productive dialogue in the future is more appropriate now than in any other time this past half century.

Samuel P. Huntington
Eaton Professor of the
    Science of Government
Harvard University

D. Gale Johnson
Eliakim Hastings Moore
    Distinguished Service Professor
    of Economics Emeritus
University of Chicago

William M. Landes
Clifton R. Musser Professor of
    Economics
University of Chicago Law School

Sam Peltzman
Sears Roebuck Professor of Economics
    and Financial Services
University of Chicago
Graduate School of Business

Nelson W. Polsby
Professor of Political Science
University of California at Berkeley

Murray L. Weidenbaum
Mallinckrodt Distinguished
    University Professor
Washington University

Research Staff

Claude E. Barfield
Resident Fellow

Walter Berns
Adjunct Scholar

Douglas J. Besharov
Resident Scholar

Robert H. Bork
John M. Olin Scholar in Legal Studies

Anthony R. Dolan
Visiting Fellow

Dinesh D'Souza
Research Fellow

Nicholas N. Eberstadt
Visiting Scholar

Mark Falcoff
Resident Scholar

Gerald R. Ford
Distinguished Fellow

Murray F. Foss
Visiting Scholar

Suzanne Garment
DeWitt Wallace Fellow in
    Communications in a Free Society

Patrick Glynn
Resident Scholar

Robert A. Goldwin
Resident Scholar

Gottfried Haberler
Resident Scholar

Robert W. Hahn
Resident Scholar

Robert B. Helms
Visiting Scholar

Charles R. Hulten
Visiting Scholar

Karlyn H. Keene
Resident Fellow; Editor,
    The American Enterprise

Jeane J. Kirkpatrick
Senior Fellow

Marvin H. Kosters
Resident Scholar; Director,
    Economic Policy Studies

Irving Kristol
John M. Olin Distinguished Fellow

Michael A. Ledeen
Resident Scholar

Robert A. Licht
Resident Scholar

Chong-Pin Lin
Associate Director, China Studies
    Program

John H. Makin
Resident Scholar

Allan H. Meltzer
Visiting Scholar

Joshua Muravchik
Resident Scholar

Charles Murray
Bradley Fellow

Michael Novak
George F. Jewett Scholar;
Director, Social and
    Political Studies

Norman J. Ornstein
Resident Scholar

Richard N. Perle
Resident Fellow

Thomas W. Robinson
Director, China Studies Program

William Schneider
Resident Fellow

Bernard Schriever
Visiting Fellow

Herbert Stein
Senior Fellow

Irwin M. Stelzer
Resident Fellow

Edward Styles
Director, Publications

W. Allen Wallis
Resident Scholar

Sir Alan Walters
Senior Fellow

Ben J. Wattenberg
Senior Fellow

Carolyn L. Weaver
Resident Scholar

DATE DUE

MAY 0 2 1995			